Christianese 101

Christianese 101

A Lexicon for New Believers

David S. Smith

RESOURCE *Publications* • Eugene, Oregon

CHRISTIANESE 101
A Lexicon for New Believers

Resource Publications
An Imprint of Wipf and Stock Publishers
199 W. 8th Ave., Suite 3
Eugene, OR 97401

www.wipfandstock.com

PAPERBACK ISBN: 978-1-5326-4852-6
HARDCOVER ISBN: 978-1-5326-4853-3
EBOOK ISBN: 978-1-5326-4854-0

Manufactured in the U.S.A.

CONTENTS

Contents

INTRODUCTION

THE LEXICON OF THE church is confusing to those that are not a part of the culture. Given the great commission and our call to "make disciples. . ." (Matt. 28), I have thought a lot about how to explain some of the terms long time church attenders are very familiar with in a way that invites new believers into the conversation that has been going on for centuries.

This devotional includes definitions of words often used in scripture and church culture. All of the definitions are taken from the online version of Miriam-Webster's dictionary or dictionary.com. The explanations are shared for further understanding of context in scripture and culture. The goal is to ensure what is common for some is understood by all.

A friend of mine once said "the creation of culture begins with a common language." The culture of Christianity is one wrought with history and tradition. Given the number of conversions occurring around the world daily, I believe it is important to introduce everyone to the words that mean so much to our faith. Consider this work that introductory resource, one that will assist you in your journey towards a closer walk with God.

Welcome to the conversation!

SAVED

To rescue from harm, danger, or loss; To set free from the consequences of sin; redeem; To keep in a safe or healthy condition:

SAVED. IT IS ANOTHER term for being born again. There are layers to this term, however. It can be used in all tenses; past present and future.

In the past tense, the word Saved means that God provided a way for you to be "free from the consequences of sin". It means you have access to relationship with God through Christ because of the Cross. Once you are born again (see 'Born Again').

In the present tense, this word means God, through the work of the Holy Spirit, is constantly doing the work of saving you from one thing or another. The bible speaks of the work of the spirit like this:

"When the Spirit of truth comes, he will guide you into all the truth, for he will not speak on his own authority, but whatever he hears he will speak, and he will declare to you the things that are to come." (John 16:13)

The future tense of this word is eschatological. That just means it refers to the end times. When we die, the bible speaks of places where our souls will live forever. The person that is born again will live in heaven with God. The person that does not accept the sacrifice of Christ, will spend eternity separated from God.

The significance of this word is paramount. Whether referred to in the past, present or future, there is a need for understanding and acceptance of the meaning of the word and work done to make that meaning available to believers in Christ.

Prayer: Lord, thank you for saving me. Thank you for making a way for me to be free from the consequences of sin. Thank you for keeping me safe from distraction and destruction. Thank you for keeping me from an eternity in Hell. Thank you for saving me. Amen.

Scripture: Romans 10:9

Faith

Strong belief or trust in someone or something.

Faith in the age of science is something that many people struggle to come to. As we approach life as a scientist, we approach it with an assurance that we will have or find the answer to whatever question we pose. We approach it with a mindset that everything can either be proven either true of false. This mindset, though valid in many instances, has kept millions from coming to an understanding of God's work in our world. It is by faith that we learn to trust God.

God often times tells God's people to do things that are untraceable and even crazy. God asked Noah to build an ark in the middle of a town and he had never seen rain before. God asked Abraham to leave his family and move to a new place that he'd never heard of before. God asked Moses to go to Pharaoh and demand that he let God's people go. Throughout history God has asked countless numbers of people to simply believe that God would do what God promised. And when they did, they were never disappointed.

What is God asking you to do by faith? What are you looking to prove that can't be proven but just needs to be responded to? If you act in faith, you will see God work in ways that only your faith can reveal.

Prayer: God, thank you for giving me the faith I needed to first believe in you. Thank you also for the faith to follow you each and every day. Help me to believe you and your word even when they seem to be unbelievable. Teach me to trust you more each day. In Jesus' name. Amen.

Scripture: Hebrews 11; Romans 12:3

Disciple

Someone who accepts and helps to spread the teachings of a famous person.

WHEN I THINK OF the word "disciple", the mental image is one that usually includes ancient near eastern men that were called from their occupations to follow Jesus Christ and who later were responsible for the spreading of his message around the world. With that in mind, the definition above may be offensive at first to long time churchgoers but in context, it fits pretty well.

I think it is to note that the mental image described above is often used to disqualify us from being disciples. We are obviously not Peter, James or John. Our impact on the world and individual's lives will never be as great as theirs, will it? The answer to that question may be yes or no, but we will never know until we do what they did and share the teachings of Jesus with others. The original disciples were in no way perfect people. They were people who met Jesus, learned from him and shared what they were taught. As others heard the teachings of Jesus, they were given an opportunity to make a decision to do the same; follow and share.

As you go about your day, you have many opportunities to share what God has done in your life. You can share how the teachings or example of Jesus have impacted you to be different or better. The bible and the church call this your testimony. Share it with others and see what God does. Not everyone will be as excited about what God is doing in your life as you are, but that's normal. Not everyone likes your favorite flavor of ice cream as much as you do either. It isn't your job to force your views on others. That's the work of the Holy Spirit. Just be yourself. Share your story and watch God work in other people's lives.

Prayer: God, thank you for the work you are doing and have already done in my life. I am so appreciative and so excited about it! Help me to get over the fear of sharing it with others whenever that feeling pops up. Help me to understand that me sharing my story could very well be what prompts others submit to you as I have, but don't ever let me take on that as personal pressure or as my own work. Free me to share and let me watch your hand through those words. I love you and thank you for loving and changing me. You are a wonderful God. Amen.

Scripture: Luke 14:27; John 13:35; John 15:8

Righteous

Doing, or according with, that which is right; yielding to all their due; just; equitable; especially, free from wrong, guilt, or sin; holy; as, a righteous man or act; a righteous retribution.

A PERSON THAT IS righteous is a person that just does the right thing. Often times this is where a term like righteous gets confusing. Socially and culturally, there is no longer a universally accepted definition of right and wrong. Passages of scripture such as Ezekiel 18 are prime examples of rules defined for a people in light of culture, but also endure the test of time. Verses 15-17 of The Message interpretation say a righteous man:

> "doesn't eat at the pagan shrines,
>
> doesn't worship the popular idols of Israel,
>
> doesn't seduce his neighbor's spouse,
>
> doesn't bully anyone,
>
> doesn't refuse to loan money,
>
> doesn't steal,
>
> doesn't refuse food to the hungry,

doesn't refuse to give clothes to the ill-clad,

doesn't live by impulse and greed,

doesn't exploit the poor.

He does what I say; he performs my laws and
lives by my statutes."

Some things are debatable based on the situation.
Some things are just . . . wrong.

In your pursuit of righteousness, I would like for you
to consider this list. Remember this list and realize the bible
speaks of a standard that has endured the test of time. Believers in Christ should pursue righteous lives, not for the
purposes of pride or arrogance, but so they can positively
influence those around them for the Glory of God.

Prayer: Lord God, help me remember your rules and desires for my life. As I live my life help me to make decisions
that you would say are right. Help me be righteous. It may
be difficult at times but I want to do it for you. For your
glory Lord. Amen.

Scripture: Ezekiel 18; Romans 3:10

Covenant

An agreement, usually formal, between two or more persons to do or not do something specified.

PROMISES. WE ALL MAKE them. Most times we intend to keep them. When we cannot or do not follow through on our promise it does not necessarily mean we are being dishonest with ourselves or the other party. It does, however, mean that we are well intended but unable to do what we said we would do.

Covenants are akin to promises. God is often found in scripture requesting things of us and promising something in return. When Israel found themselves in troublesome situations they were often reassured by God with words similar to this: "I will be your God and you will be my people". (Exodus 6:7; Leviticus 26:12; Jeremiah 30:22) The promise of God is communicated to the people of Israel in a way that requires them to have faith so that God could be who God said God would be. Other times the requirement on our part is trust (Proverbs 3:5), obedience (Deuteronomy 28:1), and commitment (Joshua 24:14). This is by no means an exhaustive list. It is just compiled to help paint the picture of what we are required to do in response to God's covenant with us.

Some times the response God asks for is one that we just cannot give. We want to keep our end of the bargain, but we become weak. God knew that would happen and was so faithful to ensure the covenant would not be broken, God allowed someone else to do what we could not do. Whenever we break the contract, or fail to live up to our end of the covenant, remember these simple yet powerful words from an old hymn. . . "Jesus paid it all". God loves us so much that God covered our inability through the sacrifice of Jesus on The Cross. What you can't—or sometimes just won't—do was already done for you. What a wonderful savior!

Prayer: God, thank you so much for the promise that you made to us to always be our God and for us to always be your people. Thank you for the provision you made through Jesus where even when we can't or won't be faithful to the covenant made, you are still willing to accept us because of Christ's sacrifice. Today we commit ourselves to following you again. We will do our best, and where we know we will fall short, we ask for your help and hand to intervene and make us stronger than we think we can be. Make us more like you. In Jesus name, amen.

Scripture: Exodus 6; Leviticus 26; Jeremiah 30; Proverbs 3:5; Deuteronomy 28:1; Joshua 24:14

Holy

Specially recognized as or declared sacred by religious use or authority.

THE WORD HOLY—OR HOLINESS—IS intimidating. It is often considered as a word only ascribed to God or things that God has blessed. Churches are holy. People that hold special positions in religious service, such as pastors and priests, are holy. God is holy. Though this is true, it is an incomplete contextualization of the word and concept.

The bible speaks to holiness as the goal for all believers. 1 Peter 1:16 says it very plainly . . . "You shall be holy, for I am holy" (ESV). If this is a goal for everyone that believes in Jesus, how are we to attain it? What are we even looking to attain? First, it is important to realize that because of your commitment to God through Christ, you are now "in Christ" (Romans 6:11). Second, since you are in Christ, the holiness ascribed to Jesus by God is transferred to you. For these two reasons, you have the right and responsibility to be holy.

How to be holy is often the place where we as believers get confused. As I said before, holiness seems like such a lofty goal. This, in my opinion, is because we ascribe it to people who hold special offices or follow all of the rules.

The way to holiness, however, is simple. It's relational. It's based in submission. A holy life—a holy person—is a life fully submitted to God through Christ. As you follow God closely by reading the bible and practicing spiritual disciplines (reference here), you will learn to accept your God-given identity. You are holy.

Prayer: Lord. I surrender my life to you again today. This time my surrender is not for salvation. This time, I surrender my will and desires to your will and desires. My goal is holiness. Your plan for me is holiness. Thank you for the command to "be holy". Thank you for making me holy through my relationship with you in Christ. Help me change into your image by your spirit. In Jesus' name, amen.

Scripture: 1 Peter 1:16; Hebrews 12:14

Sin

Transgression of divine law.

Sin is a difficult topic. It has become difficult because of the interpretations of the word by many people throughout history. If you ask 10 people what sin is, you will probably hear at least 8 different answers.

The easiest way to understand this word is to remember the definition above. God shared law with us through Moses. Jesus amended these in what we refer to as The Sermon on the Mount. These two versions of The Law are great places to start when trying to understand what to do and what not to do as a believer in Christ, or Christian. If you do anything that goes against the words of Jesus or the commandment of God shared through Moses, consider it sin.

A conversation about sin is never complete for a Christian without an understanding of grace and salvation. Please review those topics today or read them for the first time if you have not already done so.

Today, let's pray for understanding.

Prayer: God, this topic is sometimes confusing, but I want it to be clear to and for me. I ask you to teach me daily through our relationship what sin is. Show me as I read The Bible. Show me through your response to my thoughts, words and actions what you approve of and don't approve of. Help me to keep an open mind and heart to you as we walk together through this developmental process. Help me to be more like you. Amen.

Scripture: James 4:17; Exodus 20:2-17; Matthew 5, 6, and 7

Justified

To prove or show (something) to be just, right,
or reasonable.

The word "justified" appears 46 times in biblical text. Each time, it speaks of the right we have, or don't have, to relationship with God. Throughout the Hebrew Scriptures, there is the theme of a need for justification. A way for the Children of Israel to explain the choice God made for them to be the Chosen people. There was no reason other than God's choice and specific individuals acceptance and obedience to God's instructions.

In the Christian Scriptures, the theme of the word is focused on the work of Christ on The Cross. This sacrifice justified the Gentile's and the Jew's relationship with God. Because of what Christ did, we are now able to worship and relate to God freely. So when people ask on what you base your relationship with God, you can tell him it's all because of your in the work of Christ on The Cross.

Prayer: God, I am grateful for the ability I have to be in relationship with you. Thank you for accepting Christ's sacrifice on the cross in a way that allows me to have a reason and a right to connect with you meaningfully. Holy Spirit—Please remind me that I am justified by my faith in Christ to be in relationship with God even when I don't feel it's true. In Christ's name and because of His sacrifice. Amen.

Scripture: Romans 3 (28); 1 Corinthians 6:11

Sanctified

To set apart or declare holy; consecrate.

THIS WORD SANCTIFIED IS one that excites me. The thought and process of sanctification for the believer is so important. Once we are justified by our faith in God through Christ, we then begin the process of being set apart for God's work in the world. This process is what distinguishes the believer in Jesus from all other people in the world. Some religions set themselves apart from the rest of the world and the dominant cultures that they're surrounded by with specific clothing or practices.

The work of sanctification in Christianity is an internal work. Believers in Christ from generations past would say "things I used to do, I don't do anymore. Places I used to go, I don't go anymore." This is the evidence of sanctification.

As you interact with and encounter God, do so in a way that allows God to change you from the inside out. Learn who God says you are by reading the scriptures. Understand how God says you should act and become more like that day by day. This work of sanctification is not an immediate thing. It is a lifelong process. Embrace it as such and your relationship with God will never get stale or boring.

Prayer. God, I want to be more like you. I pray that the work of sanctification would continue in me until I no longer want to do the things that strain our relationship. Help me to identify sin in my life on a daily basis. And once it's identified, help me to stop doing it. Make me better, Lord. This is my prayer. This is my desire. Amen.

Scripture: Jeremiah 1:5; John 17:17

MINISTRY

The period of service or office of a minister or ministry.

MINISTRY IS THE ACT of serving others with the gifts and talents God has given you for the purpose of them experiencing Christ's love for them in deeper, more meaningful ways. It is something every believer is called to do.

Every person in the world has a unique set of gifts, talents and abilities that God has given them. Those gifts, talents and abilities are ours to use however we'd like to use them. Those of us who aspire to live our lives in service to God would do well to use those gifts, talents and abilities to benefit others in the name of our Lord, Jesus Christ.

In the Sermon on the Mount, Jesus admonishes us to "let our lights shine so before others, that they may see our good deeds and glorify (God) in heaven" (Matt. 5:16). This admonition is one that we would do well to remember whenever we think of the word ministry. Our good works done in the name of the Lord is our ministry. Ministry is not relegated to the church. Ministry is and should be done wherever we are and should impact those around us for the glory of God. Let your light shine!

Prayer: God, thank you for the unique set of gifts and talents you've given me to benefit the world around me in your name. I ask that you would allow me to share what you've given me with the rest of the world without fear or shame. Help me to be the best me possible so that I glorify you through my service to others. I will be careful to give your name the praise for all you've done in my life. In Jesus' name, amen.

Scripture: Luke 3:23; 2 Timothy 1:6-8; Ephesians 4:11-13

Fellowship

A company of equals or friends.

Fellowship is our ability to connect regularly with those around us who believe what we believe and aspire to live how we aspire to live. It is a gathering of like-minded individuals for the purposes of sharing the joys and struggles of life. This sharing creates a connection that goes deeper than mere friendship or camaraderie. It provides a foundation for living that helps us realize we are not alone in whatever we find ourselves in.

Fellowship for the early church was imperative. It was the means through which believers were able to strengthen themselves in prayer and conversation for a few hours a day or week as they faced a world that was completely opposed to their message. This opposition often led to persecution, ridicule, imprisonment or even death for those who were unwavering in their faith. Strength was shared in community when believers got together to pray and sing songs of praise to God for all God had done for them. Testimonies of God's faithfulness through life's challenges were shared, and everyone was reminded of the teachings of scripture.

This same strength can be found today when we gather together with like-minded believers in church services, bible studies, small group meetings and worshipful places all around the world. Living life as a believer in Jesus Christ is still not a popular decision. Being reminded that you are not alone is something we all can appreciate. The strength found in that is something we all need to engage in regularly.

Prayer: Lord, I appreciate you for sending people into my life that believe what I believe about you. Thank you for the strength we receive from each other as we praise and worship you together. I pray that you would let me encourage those around me and that you would open my eyes to the encouragement you are trying to share with me through my brothers and sisters in Christ. In Jesus' name, amen.

Scripture: 1 Corinthians 1:9; Psalm 133; Acts 2:42; Hebrews 13:16

Gospel

*The message or teachings of a religious teacher;
something accepted or promoted as infallible
truth or as a guiding principle or doctrine.*

THE GOSPEL IS THE message of Jesus Christ. In that message, the plan and hope for our salvation is shared. It is through the sacrifice of Jesus Christ on the cross of Calvary that allowed the world an opportunity to be in right relationship with God.

The Gospel is also known as the "good news". It is referred to as that because it is through the gospel message that we realize we have been forgiven of all of our sins at the moment we acknowledge and accept Jesus' sacrifice of the cross as payment for all of our transgressions. Nothing else is or ever will be required for our salvation and restored relationship with God. We cannot pay for it. We cannot work for it. All that is required is acceptance of this message as truth and appropriation of it to our lives.

I must say, that is some very good news!

Prayer: God, thank you so much for the message of salvation that I once heard which caused me to believe and accept you as my savior. I'm so grateful for the work of Christ on the cross! The testimony I have and the new life I enjoy with you is all because of this news being shared with me. Help me to be faithful to share it with others so they can feel the same joy I am feeling now. I pray this in the name of Jesus. Amen.

Scripture: Mark 16:14; Romans 8:2-6; John 3:6-8; Romans 1:16

Spirit

A supernatural being or essence.

As CHRISTIANS, WE ARE Trinitarian believers. We believe in three expressions of God, traditionally known as Father/Creator, Son/Savior, and Spirit/Guide. One of the things missing from many of our creeds and doctrinal statements is an understanding of the person and work of Holy Spirit.

The work of the Spirit in the life of the believer is a work that allows us to know what to do in the moment, saving us from distraction and destruction. It is a work that we need to yield to every day. Some call it your conscience. As believers, we call it Holy Spirit.

When I think of the work of Holy Spirit, I often point to the words of Jesus found in John 16:13 "But when he, the spirit of truth, comes, he will guide you into all truth." The work of Spirit is a work that leads us into truth. It is the work of the Spirit of God that helps us with understanding the difference between right and wrong; good, better, and best. Without the Spirit we would be left to our own devices and wisdom, which would leave us at a severe disadvantage.

Prayer: God, I thank you for sending Holy Spirit to us to lead us and guide us into all truth. I ask that you would help me yield my decisions and desires to the Spirit's leading.

Teach me how to choose what's best instead of just what seems right in my eyes. I commit to being submitted to you in all things. In Jesus' name, amen.

Scripture: John 16:13; Acts 1:8

GRACE

*Unmerited divine assistance given humans for
their regeneration or sanctification.*

THE CONCEPT OF GRACE is one of the most foundational of
concepts for the Christian. Grace is the understanding that
the work Christ did on the cross allows us to be in relationship with God. It is something we did not deserve.

We are not saved because we are good people. Christ
did not die because we are entitled to a close relationship
with God. Christ died on the cross because God wanted us
close and had no way to ensure that type of relationship
other than doing what we could not do for ourselves.

As we enjoy our walk with God and share our passion
others, it would benefit us to remember that this love that
we enjoy is a love that is given to us because God wanted
us, not the other way around. The provisions made for our
salvation were in response to God's desire for relationship
with you. Our need for God is a byproduct of God's desire
for us, not a means for us to receive and share salvation
through humility. The sooner this is understood and em-
braced, the easier and more fulfilling our walk with God
will be.

Prayer: God, thank you for the grace you have given us each day. It is your grace that found me, and it is by your grace I'm kept every day. Help me to understand that I can never work hard enough to receive your salvation. Help me to receive your grace each and every day with gladness. In the matchless name of Jesus I pray. Amen.

Scripture: Eph. 2:8-9

MERCY

*Kind or forgiving treatment of someone who
could be treated harshly.*

MERCY IS AN OPPORTUNITY for us to receive something we
do not deserve. It is not a right. It is in no way an obligation
on the part of the giver. In fact, it is just the opposite. It is
a privilege extended to someone who does not deserve it.

One of the most difficult things about mercy is receiving it. When we are given something that we know we do
not deserve, it can be difficult to accept the gift. We live in a
culture where we are required to earn whatever we receive.
That cultural norm limits our ability to fully receive the
mercy of God in our lives because we have difficulty receiving what we haven't earned with confidence.

This is where the words of the writer of Hebrews become so important. God's instructions for us are instructions that admonish us to approach God with confidence,
knowing that we will receive mercy. Without this confidence, we are at risk of misappropriating our common
salvation by making it something we have to earn instead
of a gift that is freely given. Let's not make that mistake.
Let's receive God's gift of mercy as what it is. . . a free gift

from God to us. If we work to earn it, we will forever miss the mark.

Prayer: God, I thank you for your mercy. Without it our lives would be drastically different. I thank you that your work on the cross has freed me from all sin. All. Sin. I am grateful for your mercy and I accept it today as a free gift from you. Amen.

Scripture: Psalm 149:5; Psalm 86:5; Hebrews 4:16

Convicted

To make aware of one's sinfulness or guilt.

THIS WORD IS TYPICALLY referred to when speaking of legal matters. When someone is convicted it typically means that they have been found guilty of a crime and are now being punished for it.

For Christians, that meaning is true, in part. It is true because the feelings that accompany inappropriate behavior are the same whether you break a law of society or a law of God. Where they differ is in the judgment and punishment process.

When we are convicted of sin, which is the way the term is usually used; we are plagued with an internal feeling that something is wrong that would otherwise be right. The wrong is not based on your standards for living but on God's standard. It is sometimes confused with guilt or shame, but it is actually a beautiful opportunity to more closely align yourself with the character of God.

When conviction comes, embrace it. It may seem easier to justify your actions or thoughts, but in the long run it will be better for you and those around you if you embrace the prompting and modify your behavior based on God's leading.

Prayer: Lord, I appreciate that you care enough about me to show me when and where I am not like you through your conviction power. Help me to stay free from guilt or shame. Let your conviction lead to repentance and repentance to freedom in you. I pray this for your glory and in your name, Amen.

Scripture: Romans 7

SACRIFICE

An act of killing a person or animal in a religious ceremony as an offering to please a god.

THE BIBLE WAS WRITTEN in a time when sacrifices were customarily offered to gods. The religions of Ancient Near East culture were ones that did not take issue with offering animals, or even people, in worship to their god or gods. The parent religion of Christianity, Judaism, is no different.

The first five books of the Bible, known as the Pentateuch, speak a great deal about sacrifice. There is the story of Cain and Abel where Abel offered an animal in sacrifice to God (Genesis 4). There is the story of the story of Abraham's near sacrifice of his son Isaac on an alter (Genesis 22). There are even instructions on what acceptable sacrifices are in the book of Leviticus (Leviticus 1-5).

As Christians, we no longer believe that animal sacrifices are a requirement for relationship with God. The words of the great hymn of the church written in 1865 speak to the reason why we no longer believe this:

> "Jesus paid it all,
> All to Him I owe;
> Sin has left a crimson stain,
> He washed it white as snow."

The red stain of spilled blood that was once the sign of repentance and redemption is no longer necessary. Now we are asked by God to offer our hearts (or desires) and our lives as a living sacrifice of worship (Romans 12:1-2). This is the sacrifice of the Christian's life.

Prayer: God, help me to sacrifice myself—my will and desires—for your will and desires for my life. Help me to be a person that honors you with all that I do and all that I am. Let my decisions be ones that you would be happy with. Let the sacrifice of Jesus be honored by the life I live. In your son's name, Amen.

Scripture: Genesis 22; Romans 3:25; Hebrews 9:2

Worship

Reverent honor and homage paid to God or a sacred personage, or to any object regarded as sacred.

Worship is not just a topic for the Christian community. All major world religions have a form of and rules for worship. Prayer, giving to the poor, attending gatherings with others of the same faith, developing relationships and living lives that lead to peace and harmony, and making sacrifices that require self-discipline are some of the things that are common in the practice of worship for all major world religions. The difference for the Christian is the object of our worship. Our worship is ascribed to God.

The apostle Paul shares a wonderful admonition for those of us who desire to worship God in the book of Romans. His words speak to how we ought to give God our worship. He says:

> *"Therefore, I urge you, brothers and sisters, in view of God's mercy, to offer your bodies as a living sacrifice, holy and pleasing to God—this is your true and proper worship."*

This offering of your body is all-inclusive. We have an amazing opportunity to decide to submit ourselves fully to God every moment of every day. This is worship in action—the giving of your mind (thoughts), body (desires), and emotions (feelings) to God in order to understand and live out God's perspective on and in all things. This is no easy task, but it is one that God is definitely worthy of. Will you worship today?

Prayer: God I submit my life to you. I give you my heart, my life, my thoughts, my dreams and my desires, and I pray that you would live through me. Give me your perspective on life and the world as I worship you daily . . . because you love me, and I love you. Amen.

Scripture: John 4; Romans 12:1

PRAISE

The offering of grateful homage in words or song, as an act of worship.

THE CONTEXT OF THE church's conversation on praise is most often centered on the time in the service where songs are sung in concert with other believers. These songs often have lyrics that speak to the majesty, power, provision, and our hope in and dependence on God. Though I appreciate this perspective, it leaves much to be desired for the believer when trying to understand praise from a biblical perspective.

Praise in the bible is an expression of thanks to God for all God has done for you personally and/or us collectively. It is offered at various times; after major life events (Luke 1:46-55), after God does something significant or miraculous for God's people (Exodus 15), or even in response to God's ability to share his strength with us to function daily (Psalm 146). Praise, therefore, is the opportunity for us to thank God for all we have and all we are.

Offering praise to God may feel a little weird, and rightly so. Expressions of adoration offered to another make us vulnerable. There is no reason to feel weird or ashamed for saying "thank you" to the creator of all things. Without

God, we would not exist. Without God's involvement in our lives daily, our lives would be very different. Saying "thank you" and expressing your appreciation in various ways is the least we can do for all God has done for us.

Prayer: God, thank you. Thank you for being my God and guide. Thank you for being my way maker. Thank you for your protection from situations that I knowingly entered into but also for your protection from dangers I was unaware of. Your ways and work in my life are worthy of my praise so I give it to you today. Be glorified with and through my life. In Jesus' name. Amen.

Scripture: Psalm 150; Luke 1:46-55; Exodus 15, Psalm 146; Psalm 103

LOVE

A feeling of warm personal attachment or deep affection, as for a parent, child, or friend.

LOVE IS A LOADED word. The feelings it conjures are real. The need for it is innate. Love is necessary. Whether accepted or rejected, love always requires an investment of energy, intellect and emotion.

One of the verses of scripture most quoted on this topic is 1 John 4:8b "God is love". In context, this phrase speaks of two things. First, it speaks to the need for those that love God to love the people that are in and around their lives every day. Second, it speaks of how God shows us love– through the death of God's son, Jesus, so that our sins could be forgiven. Both of these aspects of love are critical to our relationship with God.

Because love is both noun (descriptive) and verb (active), it can be confusing to identify. Sometimes the expression of love that we expect is unavailable to us. Other times, the desire for love is manipulated with actions that are untrue or insincere. This is why I believe the Bible provides a way to test the sincerity of love. It is found in 1 Corinthians 13. Verses 4 through 7 are critical to our ability to identify true love. Read and consider these verses when you are wondering if the love you are giving or receiving is true and pure based on scripture.

Prayer: God, thank you so much for loving me! Thank you for setting the standard for love through the sacrifice of Jesus on the cross. Teach me how to be loved and share love in ways that communicate your love for myself and others. I receive your love. I'd be lost without it. Amen

Scripture: John 4:8; 1 Corinthians 13

FORGIVE

To grant pardon for or remission of (an offense, debt, etc.); absolve.

FORGIVENESS IS ONE OF the most significant concepts in Christianity. It is also one of the most difficult things to do. The concept is established in the Hebrew Scriptures with the annual practice of offering sacrifices acceptable to God for the purposes of being forgiven of the sins one has committed. The establishment of feasts and festivals for the purpose of offering sacrifices to God continues throughout history and is culminated with the ultimate sacrifice: Jesus' death on the cross. From that point on, God requires no other sacrifice for forgiveness of sin other than the acceptance of Jesus.

Jesus speaks plainly on the concept of forgiveness prior to his death in the sixth chapter of the book of Matthew. This is the chapter that contains the model for prayer we often use. After teaching the disciples to pray, Jesus chooses to accentuate only one portion of the prayer; the portion on forgiveness. His words are brief, but clear: "For if you forgive men their trespasses, your heavenly father will also forgive you. But if you do not forgive men their trespasses, neither will your heavenly father forgive your trespasses." His point is this, You must forgive to be forgiven.

There are many other powerful examples of this in scripture. My desire with these words is to share with you the foundational nature of forgiveness to the Christian faith. We were forgiven by God through the sacrifice of Christ. Without that sacrifice, our worship would be in vain. Because of that sacrifice, our forgiveness must be extended to those who have offended, hurt, mistreated, abused, or otherwise harmed us; even if the offending party is you yourself. This is not negotiable. Forgiveness is a requirement.

Prayer: God, thank you for forgiving me of my sins. Thank you for the sacrifice of Christ on the cross so that I can be in relationship with you. I appreciate and am grateful for this sacrifice and accept it wholeheartedly. As I think about the requirement of forgiveness, I want to take this time to forgive any and everyone that has ever hurt, offended, misused, or otherwise negatively impacted my life in any way. I forgive them today. I also forgive myself for any inappropriate action or destructive behavior that I've engaged in prior to this day. Show me where I have hurt others or myself, and help me to extend forgiveness to me. In the name of Jesus and because of His sacrifice, Amen.

Scripture: Matthew 6:14-15; Romans 10:9-10

PRAY

*To offer devout petition, praise, thanks, etc., to
(God or an object of worship).*

PRAYER IS AN OPPORTUNITY for the believer to communicate with God. Often it is thought to be more complicated than it has to be. Simply put, prayer is a conversation between God and you.

Many are confused about how to pray or even intimidated to do so. Some of this is due to the one with whom we have been granted an audience. The magnificence of communicating with the Creator of all things is awe-inspiring, but it does not have to be intimidating. When we realize God wants to communicate with us, it should provide some assurance and consolation.

Jesus shares a model for prayer with us in Matthew 6. This model prayer is often the only prayer many believers learn to pray. Though important, I would urge you to move beyond the script and engage in a conversation with God. Use this model prayer as just that, a model to frame your thoughts and words as you talk with God. The components of the model prayer are:

- Acknowledgement of God's position.
- Acknowledgement of God's holiness.

- Acknowledgement of God's kingdom.

- Acknowledgement of God's will and our partnership with God to carry that out.

- Acknowledgment of our need for God to provide for us.

- Acknowledgement of our need to forgive and be forgiven.

- Acknowledgement of our need to be kept from temptation and evil.

- Reiterated acknowledgement of God's kingdom, power and position (glory).

- Acknowledgement of God's ever existence.

It may be difficult to cover all of these topics every time you pray, so don't force it. I suggest you pick a topic or theme for a day and focus on it. This is a conversation that will last for the rest of eternity. There is no need to feel rushed.

Prayer: God, thank you for the opportunity to talk with you. Sometimes I don't understand how or why you would want to have a conversation with me, but I am grateful for the opportunity. I ask you to do for me what you did for the disciples; teach me to pray. Help me to hear from you. Help me to be comfortable talking with you. Deepen our relationship through this conversation. Teach me more about you, myself, and others as we talk. In Jesus' name, Amen.

Scripture: Matthew 6:5-15

GIVE

To present voluntarily and without expecting compensation; bestow.

GIVING IS A HOT topic in the church these days. It is one of the most often mentioned reasons that people do not go to church. Many feel as though the church asks for money too frequently, which is a turn off. A biblical perspective on giving is one that is centered on free will. God does not want—and the church should not want—you to give something that you don't want to give. Giving is something that is done "voluntarily and with no expectation of compensation".

Every major world religion considers giving a major component of a disciplined lifestyle. The Jews believe in the 8 levels of Tzedakah. Giving, or compulsory charity, is the third of five pillars in Islam. For Hindus, Dana is practiced, which is the consistent giving for the purposes of drawing spiritual fulfillment. For the Christian, tithing and giving of offerings is practiced for the purposes of maintaining a generous heart and spirit. (See 'Tithing'. See 'Offering'.)

Giving is so important that Jesus mentions it as an assumed behavior in the greatest sermon ever preached—The Sermon on the Mount (Matthew 6-8). There are only three "when" statements in this sermon; when you give, when you pray and when you fast (Matthew 6:1-18). All of these are stated as a non-negotiable for the committed believer.

If you find yourself in a place where you feel the church is asking for too much, I challenge you to adjust your perspective. Ask yourself what God is requesting of you and do just that. Search the scriptures and your heart/mind for the answer that is a challenge to and for your faith. Then, step up to that challenge.

Prayer: God, there have been some that have not taught about giving in a way that helps me understand and embrace your instructions on the topic. For that reason, I pray today that you would re-teach me everything I need to know about giving. Remove any false teaching from my mind and heart and replace it with what is right and true. Help me to follow you in this area. In Jesus' name. Amen.

Scripture: Matthew 6:2-4; 2 Corinthians 9:7

Tithe

(n) The tenth part or any indefinitely small part of anything.

(v) to give or pay a tithe or tenth of (produce, money, etc.)

TITHING IS A DERIVATIVE of the principle of giving outlined in most major religions. It is first mentioned in the book of Genesis (Gen. 14:18-20) when Abraham gave the King of Salem and Priest of God ten percent of the wealth acquired after a victorious battle against a group of kings that had taken his nephew Lot captive.

Often times, tithing is considered an obligatory practice that some use to blame the church for being greedy. It is off-putting to many, and understandably so. Reframed in its proper context, however, the concept of giving is common to most world religions. One of the five pillars of Islam is Zakat, which is an annual gift given based on earned income. Hindu ascribes to Dasvandh, which is literally translated as "tenth giving" (dasvandh.org). Even most major corporations strongly encourage their employees to give a portion of their income to charitable causes.

As you continue to attend the church of your choosing, you will hear many reasons to tithe that are based on scripture. All of them are true. I urge you, however, to allow those reasons to be additions to a pillar of our faith, which is this; we tithe to maintain a generous heart and spirit. It is a principle of giving.

Prayer: Lord, help me to be more generous today and every day. Teach me how to trust you with what you have given me in a way that puts the needs of others before my own needs in this small, but significant way. Bless me and make me a blessing to others. In Jesus' name. Amen.

Scripture: Leviticus 27:32; Hebrews 7

Baptize

To cleanse spiritually; initiate or dedicate by purifying.

THE ACT OF BEING baptized in the Christian church holds a place of significance that not many other things hold. Purification of people and things through water was held sacred in Hebrew Scriptures. The same importance was carried over into the Christian scriptures when John the Baptist baptized Jesus in the Sea of Galilee.

Some churches require new believers be baptized before joining the church. Others recommend it as a declaration to the world and their church family once a person accepts Christ as their savior (see saved). Some believe that baptism can and should be done for babies (infants) soon after they are born. Others require that the ceremony be completed only on people that are old enough to understand what is actually happening and can explain it in their own words. No matter how it is practiced, the significance of this act is real and universally accepted by The Church. We differ on how to baptize, not on the importance of baptism.

As your relationship with God matures, I would recommend you learn more about how your church believes baptism should be conducted. As you learn, think about how you can support and align yourself with their doctrine (system of belief and practice).

Prayer: God, the longer I live, the more I want to be like Jesus. Help me to see and realize how this act can help me do just that. Help me to engage in the life of The Church and my church healthily. I submit to your will and your ways. Amen.

Scripture: Matthew 3:13-17

Repent

To feel such sorrow for sin or fault as to be disposed to change one's life for the better; be penitent.

Have you ever felt so bad about something that you couldn't shake the feeling of guilt or remorse? No matter what you did, the thoughts and feelings you were plagued by just wouldn't go away, even after an apology was shared with the person you felt you wronged. Did you ever feel the need to do something to make things better? The need to do something to try to erase the wrong somehow?

The guilt we may feel from living a sinful life. We feel guilty because we are not doing what God says we should do. (see Matthew 6-8). When a person begins their relationship with God through Jesus and realizes how they lived their life previously made God feel, it is often accompanied by a feeling of guilt and sometimes shame.

God makes us an offer to erase those feelings. That offer is summed up in one word: repent. This word for the Christian means we recognize how our thoughts and actions were not in line with God's thoughts about and desired actions for us. Once recognized, it is up to us to ask God for the strength and fortitude to "make it right" by doing what is needed to change our thoughts and behavior.

Sometimes the work of repentance is confused with working to be accepted by God. Please let me be clear. There is no way you can do anything at all to be accepted by God other than accept the sacrifice Christ made for you on the cross (see 'SAVED').

Prayer: God, I know that there are areas in my life where I did not do what you would have wanted me to do. Sometimes I knew I wasn't right. Other times, I was clueless . . . but now that I know help me to turn from those actions and live a life that honors you. In Jesus Name. Amen.

Scripture: Numbers 23:19; Ezekiel 18:30; Job 42:1-6; Joel 2:12-13; Acts 2:38

Sacrifice

An act of offering to a deity something precious.

SACRIFICE IS GIVING SOMETHING up because something else means more to you than the thing you are deciding to forego. The idea of sacrifice in Christianity is expressed in many forms, but it can be summed up in just a few words. As Christians, we sacrifice for God and to God. The expressions of sacrifice are manifold. Our time, talents, finances, goals, desires, and even our ideals are opportunities for sacrifice.

As new covenant believers, we are challenged by the Apostle Paul to present ourselves to God each day in the form of a sacrifice. By this, Paul is urging us to submit everything we are and everything we have to God in a way that says "God, these things are important to me, but I want you more." We express our hearts desire to God through our decisions. It is when we show God how much God is important to us that we truly live a life in line with Jesus. "Not my will, but yours be done" (Luke 22:42b).

Prayer: Lord, thank you for giving the ultimate sacrifice on the cross for me. Your dedication to me through such an unselfish act leads me to want to do the same for you. Teach me what and how to sacrifice for you today and every day.

Help me to submit to you as I walk through this life with my hand in yours. I pray this in Jesus' name, Amen.

Scripture: Romans 12:1

FAST

To abstain from all food; to eat only sparingly or of certain kinds of food, especially as a religious observance.

To FAST IS WHEN we sacrifice eating for some greater purpose. Most of us are familiar with fasting for medical purposes. The doctor orders us to come into the office prior to eating or drinking anything with caloric density. If you're anything like me, you try to make those appointments for as early in the morning as possible to ensure you accomplish the goal with as minimal personal impact as possible.

Fasting for the Christian is similar but the goal is different. When we fast, as Jesus says in Matthew 6:16, we are doing so to get closer to God. Our fast is a sacrifice of something necessary to us for the purpose of obtaining something of even more importance, a closer relationship with God. Fasting shows God in a tangible way that God is more important to you than life's necessities.

So when you fast, do so in a way that makes God the focus of your sacrifice. Sacrifice alone won't change a thing. It is the desire to give up something to get closer to God that produces results.

Prayer: Lord, thank you for the many examples of sacrifices you've made for me. I willingly accept your call to fast to get closer to you. As I do so, help me remain focused on our relationship. Draw me closer to you. In Jesus' name, amen.

Scripture: Matthew 6:16; 1 Corinthians 7:5; Daniel 10:3; Esther 4:16

Altar

An elevated place or structure, as a mound or platform, at which religious rites are performed or on which sacrifices are offered to gods, ancestors, etc.

Altars have a special place in scripture. They first appearance of the word is found in the story of Noah and the Ark. After the water subsided and Noah realized he and his family were saved from the flood, he exited the ark and built an altar to sacrifice an offering of thanksgiving to God. This place Noah built was a place that was created specifically for the purpose of worshiping God.

Since Jesus' sacrifice on the cross we no longer have to offer sacrifices as they did in the days of Ancient Israel. Instead we offer our lives in submission to Christ every day. Paul speaks to this in Romans 12 when he admonishes us to present ourselves as a living sacrifice to God. With the requirement to offer additional sacrifices for the forgiveness of sin, it is our duty and right to offer ourselves in sacrifice to the God of our salvation.

Prayer: God, thank you that we no longer have to use an altar of sacrifice to reconnect with you. Thank you that your work through Christ on the cross was, is, and forever will be enough to offer us daily forgiveness from sin. I pray that as I go through this day that you would remind me that I am now the sacrifice you seek. Accept my offering; my life submitted to you. In Jesus' name. Amen.

Scripture: Genesis 8:20; Genesis 12:7; Genesis 26:25

HEAVEN

The dwelling place of the Deity and the blessed dead.

HEAVEN IS THE PLACE that is typically referred to as God's dwelling place. It is the eternal home of those who have died in faith and now rest with God.

Heaven is a comforting thought to those of us who have lost loved ones. I've often heard it said when someone dies "they're in a better place". This is true for those of us who die after having accepted Jesus as our Lord and Savior. We are no longer burdened by the struggle and shame of our sin, the frailty of our bodies, or the limitations of our minds. We are with God for all eternity! I can't think of anywhere else I'd rather be.

John the Revelator described the beauty of heaven in Revelation 21. Jesus spoke of our personal space reserved by him for us in heaven in the 14th chapter of the book of John. Paul spoke of heaven as a reward for the believer in the first chapter of his book to the Philippian church. He also spoke of the reality of heaven in the 15th chapter of 1 Corinthians. All of these passages of scripture give us a different understanding of what life forever in the presence of God will be like. It is these and other passages that keep me from fearing death. Life is sweet and my loved ones' precious, but the alternative of being in the presence of God for all eternity is one that I am looking forward to!

Prayer: God I thank you for caring enough about me to make room for me in your home. The promise of being with you forever is such a sweet reward that I am and will forever be grateful for. Help me to shake the fear of death. Help me to live this life in a way that reminds me always of your reward for me.

Scripture: Isaiah 25:8-12; Matthew 5:17-20; Colossians 3:1-7

Hell

*The nether realm of the devil and the demons
in which condemned people suffer everlasting
punishment.*

HELL IS A TOPIC that has kept many people away from church. It has been used by many as a scare tactic for salvation. In reality, hell is the place where one is eternally separated from God. There is no opportunity for interaction or relationship with God. It is the place reserved for those who do not accept the free gift of salvation extended to us through the sacrifice of Christ on the cross.

Controversy about hell has surrounded the church for centuries. Questions about the reality of hell as it relates to biblical context have fostered thoughts that promote hell as a historical place in time that was never a reality for life after death. The Bible teaches in no uncertain terms, however, that separation from God is a reality for those that do not receive God's love.

Hell is referred to in scripture by many names: hell, the second death, sheol, the lake of fire, and eternal damnation. Whatever name you chose, the message is still the same; separation from God forever is a reality for those that do not accept God's love through Jesus Christ.

Prayer: God, I am so grateful that I will live with you for eternity because I accepted Jesus as my savior! Thank you so much for providing a way of escape for me and everyone else in the world through Jesus Christ. I pray that those who do not know you and/or have not accepted you as their savior will do so now! Let them receive your love and live with you forever also! For your glory, Lord! Amen.

Scripture: Matthew 25:46; Revelation 21:8; Proverbs 15:24